# THE BRAILLE TRAIL

# An Activity Book

### Anna Swenson
### Frances Mary D'Andrea

**PRESS**
NEW YORK

The Braille Trail: An Activity Book    ISBN 0-89128-854-6

The Braille Trail project was made possible by a generous grant from the UPS Foundation.

Charcoal portrait of Louis Braille on p. 26, entitled **Louis Braille ". . . to open the eyes of the blind" (Isaiah 42:7)**, by Nancy Lucas Williams, copyright © 1998. All rights reserved. Courtesy of Louis Braille Center, Edmonds, Washington.

The American Foundation for the Blind—the organization to which Helen Keller devoted more than 40 years of her life—is a national nonprofit whose mission is to eliminate the inequities faced by the ten million Americans who are blind or visually impaired. Headquartered in New York City, AFB maintains offices in Atlanta; Chicago; Dallas; Huntington, West Virginia; San Francisco, and a governmental relations office in Washington, DC.

The Braille Bug and the Braille Bug symbol are registered trademarks of the American Foundation for the Blind.

Book design by Stephen D'Andrea. Braille Bug illustration created in collaboration with Justin Winslow.

# Hi! My name is Karl, and I am 12 years old.

My family lives in New Hampshire. I am a big brother to two sisters, Erika and Britt. Computers are my favorite things, and I love computer games. I also like to ski, bike, swim, jump on my trampoline and go camping with the Boy Scouts. In school I like math and science, and I play the saxophone in the band. I guess I am no different from you, except I am blind and have been since I was born.

When you started learning the print ABC's, I learned them in braille. My mom made up flashcards with bingo chips so I could feel the dots. Once I got the hang of reading braille, it was fun and easy. By the time I was six, I was reading any braille books I could get, and I could do all my school work in braille. Fantasy stories like the Harry Potter books are my favorites. I like braille because it is quick and easy to use, and I can even read in the dark! Now I have a braille notetaker that I use in class to take notes and do my school work. It's like a small laptop computer with six keys and a space bar for writing braille, but no screen. There's a picture of one on the Braille Technology pages in this book. The notetaker speaks everything I write and shows one line of braille at a time for me to read. I can even read a whole book on disk with it. I also get fun adventure games off the Internet that I can put on my braille notetaker and play (without my teacher knowing).

I think it would be a lot of fun for you to learn some braille. Some of my classmates have tried and thought it was like a secret code. They had fun seeing their names written in braille, too. With this book you can try some braille and surprise your friends with their names in braille. Or, you can find a blind friend like me to be your pen pal. I hope you enjoy learning braille. **Good Luck! Have Fun! Karl Belanger**

*I've loved reading books since I was little.*

Photo courtesy of National Braille Press

1

# Braille: Deciphering the Code

When you first look at something written in braille, all you see (or feel) is a jumble of dots! However, like any other code, braille is based on a logical system. Once you understand it, you'll be able to read and write braille easily. That's because braille is not a language, it's just another way to read and write English (or any other language, such as Japanese).

Every character in the braille code is based on an arrangement of one to six raised dots. Each dot has a numbered position in the braille cell. These characters make up the letters of the alphabet, punctuation marks, numbers, and everything else you can do in print.

$$1 \bigcirc \bigcirc 4$$
$$2 \bigcirc \bigcirc 5$$
$$3 \bigcirc \bigcirc 6$$

## The Braille Cell

- The letter "a" is written with only dot 1.

- The letter "d" has dots 1, 4, and 5.

- The letter "y" has dots 1, 3, 4, 5, and 6.

- A period is written with dots 2, 5, and 6. (Do you see how it is the same shape as the letter "d," only lower down in the cell?)

- When all six dots are used, the character is called a "full cell."

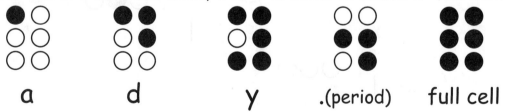

a      d      y      .(period)      full cell

The next page shows you how the dots are arranged in the braille cell for each letter of the alphabet. See if you can find the letters in your name and tell the dot numbers for each one.

# The Braille Alphabet

a  b  c  d  e  f  g  h  i  j

k  l  m  n  o  p  q  r  s  t

u  v  w  x  y  z

## The Braille Cell

1  2  3  4  5  6

Braille does not have a separate alphabet of capital letters as there is in print. Capital letters are indicated by placing a dot 6 in front of the letter to be capitalized. Two capital signs mean the whole word is capitalized.

Capital sign ⟶ ⠠⠅⠁⠗⠇
K a r l

⠠⠠⠎⠞⠕⠏
S T O P

Braille numbers are made using the first ten letters of the alphabet, "a" through "j," and a special number sign, dots 3, 4, 5, and 6.

⠼⠁  ⠼⠃  ⠼⠉  ⠼⠙  ⠼⠑  ⠼⠋  ⠼⠛  ⠼⠓  ⠼⠊  ⠼⠚

1    2    3    4    5    6    7    8    9    0

Larger numbers only need one number sign. The comma in braille is dot 2.

346 = ⠼⠉⠙⠋          1,428,300 = ⠼⠁⠂⠙⠃⠓⠂⠉⠚⠚

The next page shows the braille alphabet and the numbers without the blank dots, more like they would look on a braille page.

# The Braille Alphabet

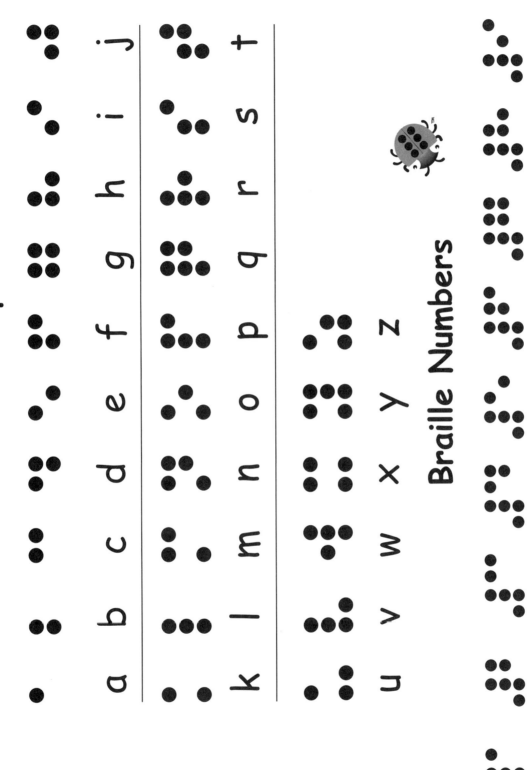

a b c d e f g h i j

k l m n o p q r s t

u v w x y z

# Braille Numbers

1 2 3 4 5 6 7 8 9 0

# How Sensitive Are Your Fingers?

When kids are learning braille in kindergarten, their teachers make worksheets to help them recognize different braille characters. Here is one for you to try. You'll need one of the braille pages that came with this book. Don't "peek" at the braille with your eyes! Just read the directions below, close your eyes and use your fingers to do the exercises on the braille page.

1.  Warm-up exercise: At the top of the page you will feel a long thick line of full cells like this:

    ⠿⠿⠿⠿⠿⠿⠿⠿⠿⠿⠿⠿⠿⠿⠿⠿⠿⠿⠿⠿⠿⠿⠿⠿⠿

    Place the fingers of both hands at the beginning of the line, with the index fingers touching. Move your fingers slowly across the page. Try to use a light touch and keep all fingers on the line. Once you can do this, try the next line which is much thinner.

    •• •• •• •• •• •• •• •• •• •• •• •• •• •• •• •• •• •• ••

2.  Below the thin line are short lines of 4 braille characters like this:

    ⠦   ⠦   ⠒   ⠦

    Three of the characters are the same. Can you find the one that is different? You will feel a long thin line of dots at the end of this exercise.

    •• •• •• •• •• •• •• •• •• •• •• •• •• •• •• •• •• •• ••

3.  The last exercise is made up of longer lines of braille characters like this:

    ⠊    ⠦   ⠊   ⠊   ⠦   ⠦   ⠊

    Feel the first character in the row. Then see how many of the other characters are the same. There will be more than one. You might like to keep your left index finger on the first character while your right hand examines the rest of the row.

## Ready? Now close your eyes and begin!

# Follow the Braille Trails

Try this!

Follow the trails and read the braille to find the messages.
Each sentence begins with a capital letter.

Path 1

Path 2

Path 3

Message 1: ___ ___ ___ ___ ___ ___   ___ ___ ___   ___ ___ ___ ___.

Message 2: ___   ___ ___ ___ ___ ___ ___   ___ ___   ___ ___ ___ ___ ___.

Message 3: ___ ___ ___ ___ ___   ___ ___ ___ ___ ___   ___ ___ ___.

Answers on page 40

 7

Now that you understand how dots are arranged in the braille cell to make the letters of the alphabet and numbers, you're ready to learn more about the code. Braille uses special characters called contractions to make words shorter. We use contractions like "don't" as a short way of writing two words, such as "do" and "not." In braille there are many additional contractions, 189 in all! Using these contractions saves space, which is very important because braille books are much larger and longer than print books.

- Some contractions stand for a whole word:

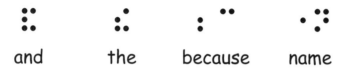

|  and  |  the  |  because  |  name  |

- Other contractions stand for a group of letters within a word:

|  ing  |  ed  |  ation  |  ound  |

In addition to contractions, the braille code includes short-form words, which are abbreviated spellings of common longer words.

tm (tomorrow)    rcv (receive)    brl (braille)

You might think that because short-form words are so easy to spell that children who write braille get a break on their spelling tests. Actually, braille readers also learn regular spelling for typing on a computer.

Let's see what kind of difference contractions make in braille. Look at the same riddle in uncontracted braille (sometimes called "grade 1 braille") and contracted braille (sometimes called "grade 2 braille"). What do you notice about the length of the two riddles?

**Uncontracted braille:**

W h a t     b o w     c a n     n e v e r     b e     t i e d ?

**Contracted braille:**

Wh a    t    b    ow   can   n   ever   be   t   i   ed ?

(For more riddles, see page 17. Answers are on page 40.)

One more comment about braille. People sometimes ask if it would be easier to use raised-print alphabet letters, rather than dots. When you read about Louis Braille on page 26 of this book, you'll learn that raised-print letters were tried in the early 1800s before he invented braille. However, these letters were very difficult to read by touch, and writing them was even more of a problem.

If you ever see an experienced reader's fingers gliding across a page of braille at 100–200 words per minute, you will appreciate the genius of the simple six-dot system. Braille can be read and written with ease by both children and adults. It is an invention that is truly here to stay.

# Other Braille Codes

The braille code used for writing regular text in books, magazines, school reports, and letters is known as "literary braille." There are other codes, though, that let people who are blind write just about anything, from music notes, to math problems, to computer notation!

## The Music Code

In addition to inventing the literary braille code for reading and writing, Louis Braille also developed a music code to help him teach his piano students at the school where he lived and worked.

In France, the first note of the musical scale was called "do." The scale continued with "re, mi fa, sol, la, ti, do." Louis Braille represented the first note of the scale with the braille letter "d" for "do" and continued the rest of the notes with the letters e, f, g, h, i, and j. In America, we call the first note of the scale "C."

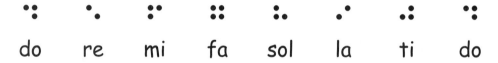

do    re    mi    fa    sol    la    ti    do

In print, musical notes are written on lines called a staff. In braille, the staff is not needed because the notes themselves change to show the musician the rhythm and pitch of the music they are playing.

Dots 3 and 6 show the rhythmic value of each note.

- Quarter note: Add dot 6 to a note.

quarter note C ⠐⠱    quarter note A ⠐⠪

- Half note: Add dot 3 to a note.

half note C ⠐⠻    half note A ⠐⠲

- Whole note: Add dots 3 and 6 to a note.

whole note C ⠐⠽    whole note A ⠐⠺

- Eighth note: No dot 3 or dot 6.

eighth note C ⠐⠙    eighth note A ⠐⠊

Here are the braille notes for the beginning of "Yankee Doodle." There is a space between each measure. Can you identify all the quarter notes? Where do you see some half notes?

# The Math Code

Most elementary school students begin learning the "Nemeth Code" for braille mathematics when they are in kindergarten or first grade. Numbers are written in the lower part of the braille cell, and there are rules about when to use the number sign and when it can be left out.

| | 1 | 2 | 3 | 4 | 5 |
|---|---|---|---|---|---|
| Literary braille: | ⠼⠁ | ⠼⠃ | ⠼⠉ | ⠼⠙ | ⠼⠑ |
| Nemeth braille: | ⠼⠂ | ⠼⠆ | ⠼⠒ | ⠼⠲ | ⠼⠢ |

Students also learn the braille symbols for mathematical signs so they can do different kinds of math problems. Which ones look like the symbols you are familiar with in print?

+ ⠖          − ⠤          × ⠦          ÷ ⠌

= ⠿          > ⠂⠄          < ⠄⠂

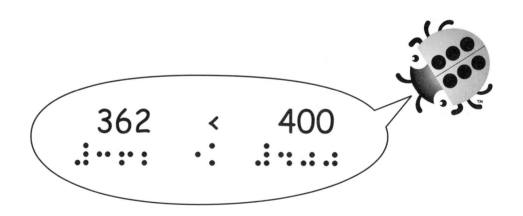

362   <   400

Here is an addition problem in braille, written both horizontally and vertically. Notice that the number sign is not used when the problem is written vertically. That's one of the rules students learn in first grade.

42 + 27 = 69

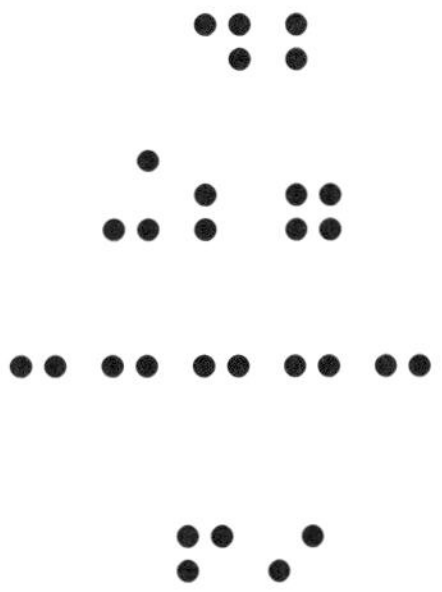

$$\begin{array}{r} 42 \\ +27 \\ \hline 69 \end{array}$$

Here's a more complicated multiplication problem for older students. It's written vertically with no number signs. Can you find the multiplication sign?

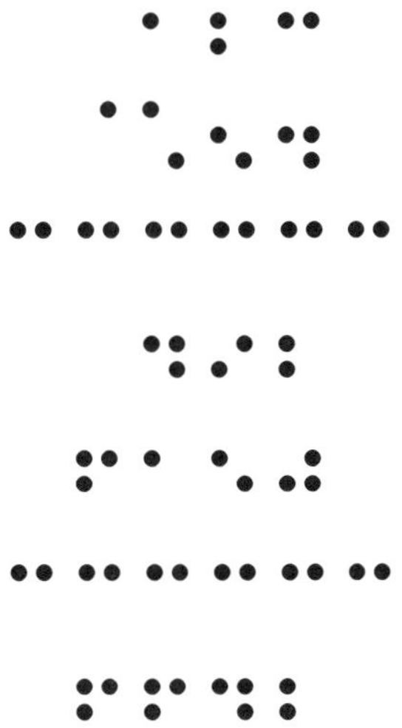

$$\begin{array}{r} 123 \\ \text{X } 54 \\ \hline 492 \\ 6150 \\ \hline 6642 \end{array}$$

# Tactile Graphics

In addition to braille, students use raised-line diagrams that they can feel when they are doing geometry, graphing, and other kinds of math. These are called "tactile graphics." Teachers of students who read braille often make tactile graphics that look like the diagrams the sighted students are using. One easy way to make a raised line is to squeeze a line of glue or "puff paint" on the diagram. When it dries, the glue forms a hard line that can be felt. Teachers also make raised lines by gluing pipe cleaners or yarn to the page.

How would you adapt the diagram below so a student who was blind could understand it? Can you think of other ways to make a tactile graphic? What might you use to show the points on the lines?

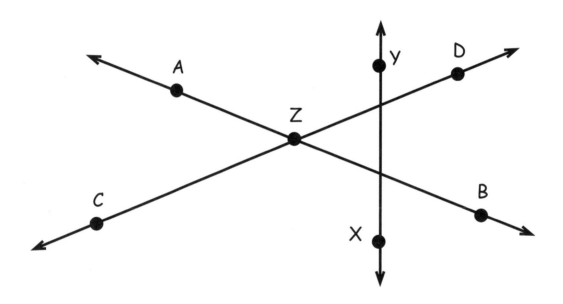

Although many teachers use art materials to make tactile graphics for their students, there are now machines that will produce raised-line copies of drawings and diagrams. Simple drawings are put on a special type of paper. The paper goes through the machine, which makes the design "puff up" so that students can feel it.

Make compound words by matching the word
on the right with one on the left.

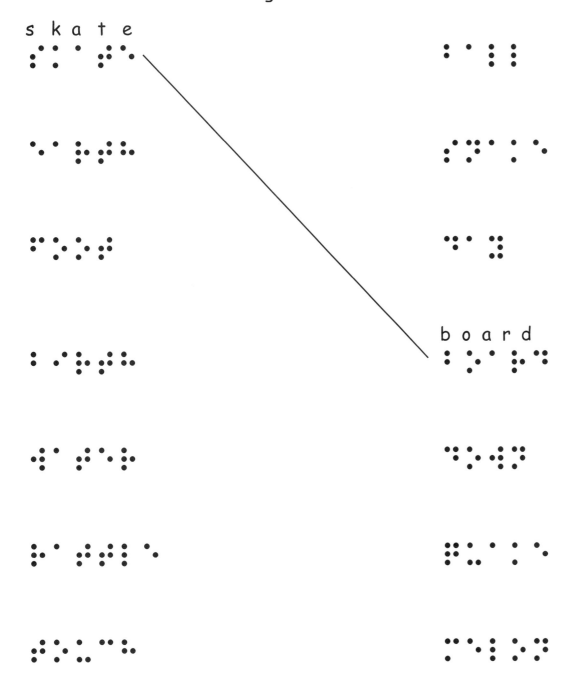

s k a t e

b o a r d

Answers on page 40

15

# Sports Scramble

Unscramble the names of the sports. Which ones do you think are played by people who are blind?

1.  ⠀⠀⠀⠀⠀⠀⠀⠀  _____

2.  ⠀⠀⠀⠀⠀⠀⠀⠀⠀  _____

3.  ⠀⠀⠀⠀⠀⠀⠀⠀  _____

4.  ⠀⠀⠀⠀⠀⠀  _____

5.  ⠀⠀⠀⠀⠀  _____

6.  ⠀⠀⠀⠀⠀⠀⠀  _____

7.  ⠀⠀⠀⠀⠀⠀⠀⠀  _____

8.  ⠀⠀⠀⠀⠀⠀  _____

9.  ⠀⠀⠀⠀⠀⠀⠀  _____

(You may not recognize this last sport. It is only for blind players.)

Answers on page 40

Try this!

1. What bow can never be tied?

⠀⠀⠀⠀⠀⠀⠀⠀⠀⠀⠀⠀⠀⠀⠀⠀

2. What time can you spell the same backward and forward?

3. How can you make seven even?

4. What school do you have to drop out of in order to graduate?

5. What do you get if you cross an insect and a rabbit?

   Capital sign ⟶

6. What runs around school all day and lies down all night with its tongue hanging out?

7. What can you add to a bucket of water that makes it weigh less?

8. Why can't a bicycle stand up by itself?

9. What contains more feet in winter than in summer?

10. How can you go out of the room with two legs and come back with six?

Answers on page 40

Try this!

# Write Your Name in Braille

Write the letters of your name on the lines. Then fill in the dots for your name in braille.

The capital sign is already done for you.

Show the braille dots for another word. How many letters do you know from memory?

TM

Try this!

# Write a Note to a Friend

Write a note in simulated braille! (sometimes called "simbraille")
Remember the capital sign and leave a blank cell between words.

Modern technology has made many useful tools for people who read and write braille. There are some devices that produce books in braille and others that let people read information on computers and from the Internet. Some devices are simple and inexpensive and others are very complicated. The devices shown here are used by many people who read braille to complete their schoolwork, take care of personal business, and do their jobs at work.

## Slate and Stylus

The slate and stylus is an inexpensive, portable tool used to write braille—just the way paper and pencil are used for writing print. Slates are made of two flat pieces of metal or plastic held together by a hinge at one end. The slate opens up to hold paper. The top part has rows of openings that are the same shape and size as a braille cell. The back part has rows of indentations in the size and shape of braille cells. The stylus is a pointed piece of metal with a plastic or wooden handle. The stylus is used to punch or emboss the braille dots onto the paper held in the slate. The indentations in the slate prevent the stylus from punching a hole

Photo courtesy of American
Printing House for the Blind

in the paper when the dots are embossed. Slates and styluses come in many shapes and sizes.

This man uses a slate and stylus at work to take notes.

Photo courtesy of American Printing House for the Blind

# Braillewriter

Braillewriters are machines that are used to write or "emboss" braille. They come in both manual and electric models. Six keys on the braillewriter represent the six dots in the braille cell. The other keys include the space bar, the back space, and the line advance (to get to the next row). Thick paper is rolled into the braillewriter and the user presses down one or more of the keys to emboss the braille.

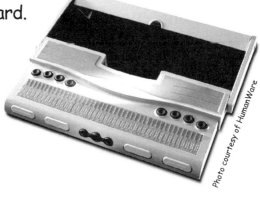

A braillewriter allows this student to check his work immediately.

# Braille Displays

A braille display is a device that has a row of special braille cells made of plastic or metal pins. The pins are controlled by a computer and move up or down to display, in braille, the characters that appear on the computer screen. This type of braille is said to be "refreshable," because it changes as the user moves around on the screen. The braille display usually sits under the computer keyboard.

Using a refreshable braille display, this student can read, write, and edit text on the computer screen.

# Electronic Braille Notetakers

Electronic braille notetakers are portable devices with braille keyboards that braille readers can use to enter information. The text stored in these devices can be read with a built-in braille display, or the device can read aloud with a synthesized voice. These devices are handy for taking notes in class, and often have built-in address books, calculators, and calendars. Notetakers can also be connected to computers so that text can be displayed and printed out.

A young student brailles a book report on her notetaker while a classsmate listens to the synthesized voice.

# Braille Printers (Embossers)

Braille printers are devices connected to a computer that do the actual embossing of braille onto thick (heavyweight) paper. They work like a regular computer printer does, in that the user can print out letters, reports, and other files from the computer.

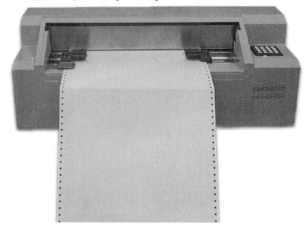

An embosser is a computer printer that prints braille.

# Write Your Own Braille with a Slate & Stylus

Have you already filled in the dots to show your name in braille on the activity sheet on page 18? Perhaps you've even "written" a note to a friend in simulated braille on page 19. You know, of course, that braille readers wouldn't be able to read the dots you've made; the dots have to be raised so they can feel them.

If you'd like to write real braille words that could be read by someone who is blind, you need to use a slate and stylus, a braillewriter, or a computer with a braille embosser. But unless you have hundreds of dollars to spend, the slate and stylus are the tools for you. There are several types of slates available. Each comes with a stylus. Two of the least expensive and easiest to use are available from the American Printing House for the Blind. To order one, you can write or call the American Printing House for the Blind.

**American Printing House for the Blind**
**1839 Frankfort Avenue, Louisville, KY 40206.**

The phone number is 800-223-1839.

- 28-cell Plastic Pocket Slate, catalog no. 1-00080-00. This 4-line slate is the width of a regular sheet of notebook paper. $6.00

- 19-cell Janus Interline Slate, catalog no. 1-00050-00. This 11-line slate holds a 3 x 5-inch index card. $5.00

## Directions for using the Pocket Slate

1. The 28-cell Pocket Slate is easy to use. Open your slate on a flat surface so that the half with holes is on the left and the half with the indentations is on the right.

2. The right half has four pins, one in each corner. Place the top edge of your paper just under the pins at the top edge of the slate, and line up the left side of the paper with the hinge.

3. Now close the left half (with the holes) firmly over the right half. You should hear a "crunch" as the bottom pins poke through the paper.

## Directions for using the Janus slate

1. Slide an index card into the Janus slate on the open side, and you're ready to write!

2. When you fill up one side, you can turn the slate over and write on the other side.

## Directions for writing braille with a slate

1. Look at the shape of each hole. It should remind you of a braille cell with a place for each of the six dots.

2. Here's the trick: You want to punch holes that you can feel on the other side of the paper. Therefore, you have to write your first letter in reverse, starting in the cell farthest to the right on the first row. Keep writing from right to left so that when you turn the paper over, the dots can be read from left to right.

3. It's easy once you get the hang of it. Use the "Reverse Braille Alphabet" on the next page to help you punch the correct dots for each letter.

4. Don't forget to leave an empty cell between words!

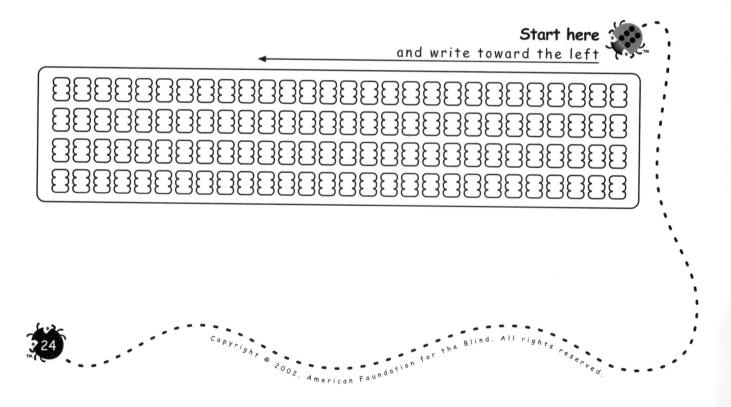

Start here
and write toward the left ←

# Tebahpla Elliarb Eht
## (for slate writing)

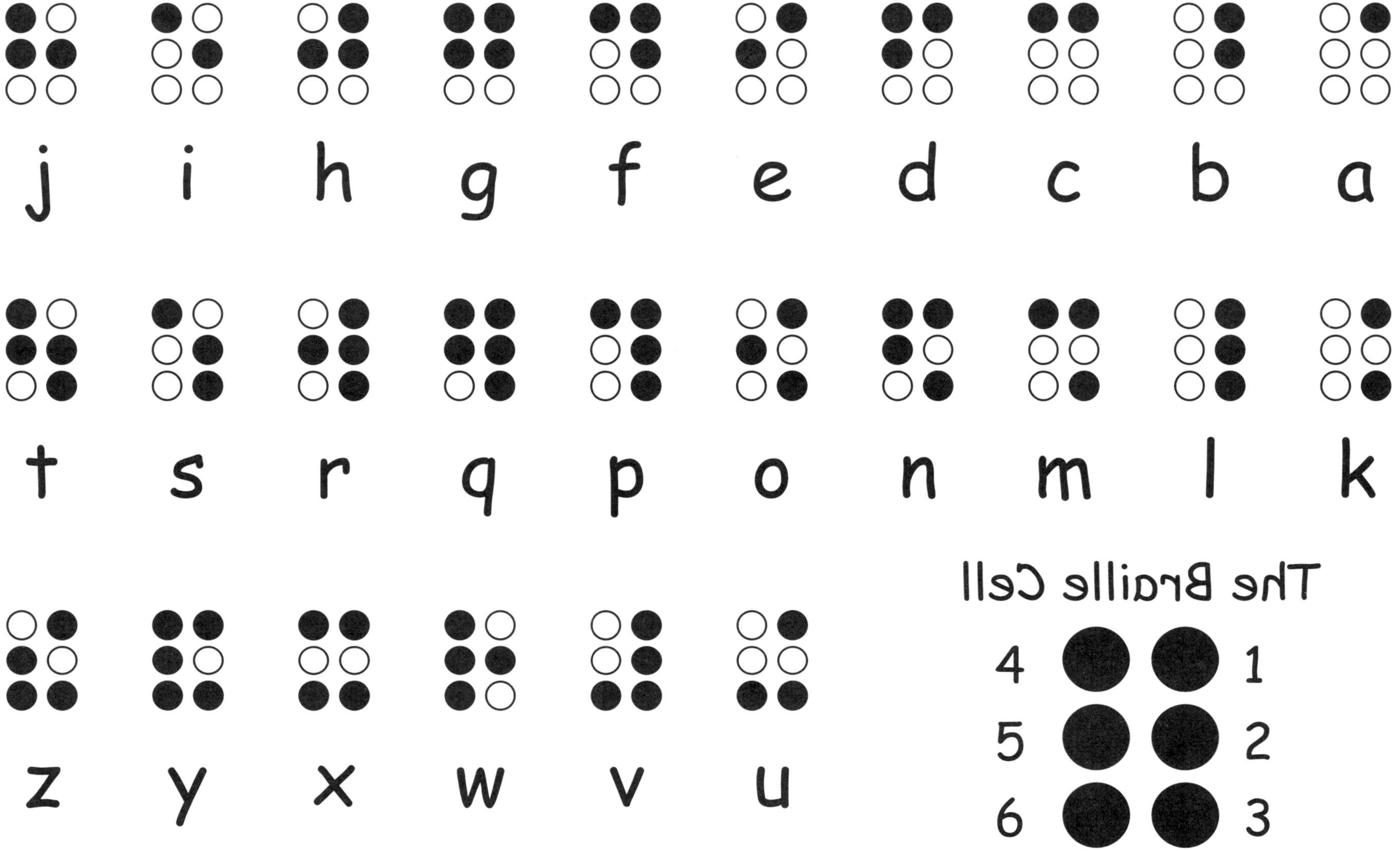

a  b  c  d  e  f  g  h  i  j

k  l  m  n  o  p  q  r  s  t

u  v  w  x  y  z

**The Braille Cell**

1  2  3

4  5  6

When you think about braille, two famous people may come to mind: Louis Braille, the inventor of the braille code, and Helen Keller, who was both blind and deaf. Read the next few pages for an introduction to their extraordinary lives and achievements. Then, if you'd like to learn more, turn to "More Reading" on page 34, which lists several biographies about Louis Braille and Helen Keller.

## Louis Braille (1809-1852)

*A pattern of tiny raised dots for each letter of the alphabet . . . . Such a simple, yet brilliant, idea that made reading possible for people who were blind. Louis Braille created his code with a flash of inspiration followed by years of hard work and determination. Why were reading and writing so important to him?*

Charcoal Portrait by Nancy Lucas Williams, courtesy of the Louis Braille Center

This drawing was made from a statue of Louis Braille

Louis Braille was born in a French village near Paris almost 200 years ago. His father was a harness maker. One day, 3-year-old Louis found a sharp tool in his father's workshop. While he was playing, it suddenly slipped and poked one of his eyes. Soon both eyes were infected, and Louis became totally blind.

In those days, most children who were blind did not attend school. However, Louis was bright and eager to learn, so the local schoolteacher allowed him to sit in the classes and listen. To everyone's surprise, Louis was able to recite his lessons from memory. He worked hard and rose to the top of the class.

At the age of 10 Louis received a scholarship to the Royal Institution for Blind Youth in Paris. He studied music and became a talented organist. Louis was frustrated in his classes because there was no easy way he and his classmates could read and write. The school had a few enormous books with raised-print letters, but these were difficult to read by touch, and writing raised letters was nearly impossible.

One day a military captain visited the school to demonstrate a complicated code of raised dots called "night writing" that his soldiers used to communicate in the dark. Louis was fascinated by this new idea. For three years he worked to arrange the dots for reading and writing quickly. Louis simplified the military code and invented the six-dot cell that would fit under a single fingertip. Then, at the age of 15, he created the reading and writing system we know today as the braille code.

The students loved Louis's new alphabet, but it took many years for the teachers and directors of the school to accept it. Louis became an instructor at the school and continued to work on his writing system. Sadly, he died of tuberculosis in 1852, at the age of 43. Two years later, France adopted braille as the official reading and writing system for blind people, and other countries followed the lead. Today, the braille code, invented by Louis Braille when he was only a teenager, is used by thousands of people around the world.

Helen Keller reading a book

## Helen Keller (1880-1968)

*We use our senses, especially vision and hearing, to know what is going on in the world around us and to communicate with others. Imagine what life must have been like for Helen Keller who was unable to see or hear! How did she learn about words and ideas?*

Helen Keller was born in Tuscumbia, Alabama, in 1880. When she was nearly 2 years old, a serious illness left her blind and deaf. Because she was deaf-blind, Helen had no way to communicate her thoughts and needs to others and became a frustrated and angry child. To make matters worse, her parents spoiled their daughter because they felt sorry for her.

When Helen was 7 years old, a teacher named Anne Sullivan came to live with the Kellers. Annie was visually impaired herself and knew how important it was for Helen to learn and become more independent. At first Helen fought wildly with the new teacher; she even locked her in her room and hid the key! Annie did not give up. She insisted that Helen behave, so that she could learn. Annie also began using sign language with her student, teaching her to spell many different words with her fingers.

For many months, sign language was just a finger game for Helen. Then one day Annie placed Helen's hands under a stream of water gushing from an outdoor pump. She spelled the letters "w-a-t-e-r" over and over into Helen's hand. Suddenly, in that magical moment, Helen discovered words. The pattern of finger shapes Annie was spelling into her hand meant the word "water," and there was a different pattern for every object, person, and idea in the whole world. From then on, Helen could not stop learning. When Annie introduced her to braille, Helen was able to read other people's ideas and express her own thoughts by writing them down. Her braille books were another link to the world, especially comforting when those around her were too tired or busy to spell into her hand.

When Helen grew older, she took lessons to help her speak. Later she graduated from Radcliffe College and wrote many books, including **The Story of My Life**. Helen traveled around the United States and to countries all over the world, showing everyone what blind people could accomplish. She visited wounded soldiers in hospitals after World War II, and gave speeches about her experiences. She was an official spokesperson working for the American Foundation for the Blind (AFB). When she died, she left all her treasures and writings to AFB, and you can see them on AFB's web site, www.afb.org/HelenKeller.asp.

Through her life and work, Helen Keller inspired people both with and without disabilities to use their talents for the benefit of others.

# Braille Trivia

- Louis Braille was only 15 years old when he invented the braille code.

- The simple six-dot cell created by Louis Braille is used all over the world by people who read many different languages.

- Braille textbooks are provided free to students who need them. Students can purchase books in braille to read for pleasure from special companies or borrow them by mail from the Library of Congress. Books for younger children sometimes have both the print and braille text on each page so their teachers or parents can follow along and help.

- Braille takes up more space than print. A regular sixth-grade math book is 11 volumes in braille!

- Braille maps, rulers, graph paper, protractors, calendars, and many other learning tools are available through the American Printing House for the Blind (see Resources for Kids, page 32).

- People who read braille can send and receive braille materials, books, and equipment free of charge through the U.S. Postal Service.

- A braille watch is read by touch, but it doesn't have braille numbers; there's not enough room! Instead there may be a group of 3 dots or a short raised line at the 12, two dots at the 3, 6, and 9, and a single dot to mark the other numbers.

- Some of your favorite games are available in braille through companies that specialize in products for people with disabilities. These include Monopoly, Scrabble, Uno, Bingo, and playing cards.

- More braille is being used in the community, thanks to the Americans with Disabilities Act (ADA) that was passed in 1990. You might see braille numbers in elevators, braille room numbers in schools, hotels, and public buildings, and braille menus in some restaurants. Where else have you seen braille recently?

- An asteroid was recently named in honor of Louis Braille.

# Braille Word Search

Try this!

Hint: Words can be horizontal, vertical, or diagonal.

```
Z S M Q P Z Z T O N I Z B O W
M N T Q C H A R A C T E R E Z
M U N Y G O L O N H C E T E T
I M T M L Y N O T E T A K E R
Q B N L M U X T I I L G L K H
W E M B O S S E R S W I J G U
W R F C T R J W K A T J H D P
X S J O E R E P M C C T G G H
G O D G A L P H A B E T X Z O
X D N I L B L T F M F R I K M
J I N I D A E R E T U P M O C
F R A N C E B N F H U Q V A N
G R M O B L B T W G H F F G J
B Z I Y R G W E H Q N H F M J
W J S Z H L S N F G P B L I N
```

ALPHABET          DOTS            READ
BLIND             EMBOSSER        SLATE
BRAILLEWRITER     FINGERS         STYLUS
CELL              FRANCE          TACTILE
CHARACTER         NEMETH          TECHNOLOGY
COMPUTER          NOTETAKER       WRITE
CONTRACTION       NUMBERS

Answers on page 41

30

# Crossword Puzzle

## Clues

### Across

3. computers for people who are blind often do this
5. the "framework" for the placement of dots in each braille character
8. the punctuation mark made with dots 2, 5, and 6
9. the number of dots in a braille cell
11. the country where braille was invented
14. a sixth-grade math book may have this many volumes
16. the number of dots in the letter "m"
17. a sharp tool that punches dots
18. a metal frame to hold the paper when writing braille
19. an alphabet of raised dots used by the blind
20. a machine for writing braille

### Down

1. a short way of writing words or letter combinations in braille
2. the name of the braille math code
4. the inventor of the braille alphabet
6. one place where you often find braille numbers
7. this short-form word is spelled "rcv" in braille
10. the side of the slate to begin writing on
11. the parts of the body that read braille
12. this game is available in braille
13. using dot 6 before a letter makes it a _____
14. a machine that prints braille from a computer file
15. dots 3, 4, 5, and 6 are called the _____ sign

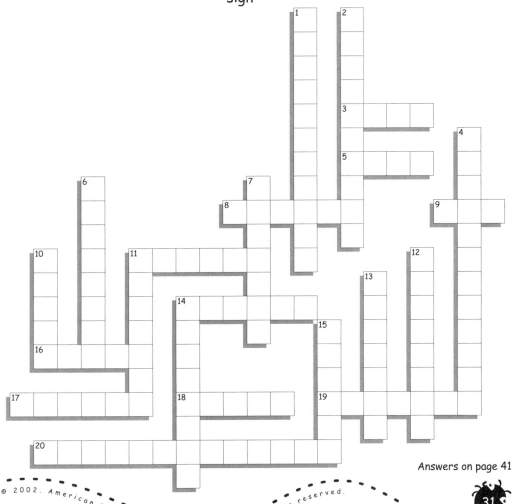

Answers on page 41

# Resources for Kids

Three great FREE resources are available from the American Foundation for the Blind:

- **Poster entitled "Braille: Dots for Reading"**
  This attractive 24 x 36-inch poster shows people of all ages using braille. You'll see a slate and stylus, an electric braillewriter, a portable braille notetaker, and other means of reading and writing braille.

- **Card with Braille Alphabet and Numbers**
  This embossed card features the Braille Bug.

- **Booklet entitled: "You Seem Like a Regular Kid to Me"**
  Meet Jane, a blind student in a regular class, and learn how she feels about her schoolwork, her friends, and her future. Lots of great photographs!

To get any of these items, write to American Foundation for the Blind, National Literacy Center, 100 Peachtree Street, Suite 620, Atlanta, GA 30303. E-mail: literacy@afb.net. Phone: 800-232-5463

## Your own copy of the special print/braille edition of "Weekly Reader"

Keep this handy to review the braille alphabet! Read about Louis Braille and try decoding the "Braille Puzzle" on the back. Available from the American Printing House for the Blind, P.O. Box 6085, Louisville, KY 40206-0085. Phone: 800-223-1839

## Braille Calendars

Several organizations will send you a free calendar in braille. Here are a few places you can get one:

Braille Institute of America, 741 N. Vermont Avenue, Los Angeles, CA, 90029; Phone: 800-BRAILLE

American Action Fund for Blind Children and Adults, 18440 Oxnard Street, Tarzana, CA, 91356

John Milton Society for the Blind, 475 Riverside Drive, Room 455, New York, NY, 10115; Phone: 212-870-3335

# Learn More about Braille on the Net!

Here are several websites about braille and blindness for you to explore.

## www.afb.org

On this website of the American Foundation for the Blind is a special area created to teach you all about braille. The site features braille games and activities introduced by our friend the Braille Bug. You can even send a "secret message" in braille to a friend! Check out www.afb.org/braillebug.

Also on the AFB website you will find a section about Helen Keller. Helen Keller became famous for her many books, articles, and speeches, and here you can read many of her writings. You will also find lots of photographs of Helen with her famous friends (such as the writer Mark Twain, the inventor Alexander Graham Bell, and President John F. Kennedy) and her personal treasures such as her Oscar award for a film about her life. Visit the Helen Keller Archives at www.afb.org/HelenKeller.asp.

## www.aph.org

APH stands for the American Printing House for the Blind which is in Louisville, Kentucky. This organization supplies many of the braille books and adapted materials that children who are blind use everyday at school. Their website includes a collection of braille writing machines from the past 125 years. There is a description and a picture of each one. Be sure to read about the Perkins Braillewriter from 1951 which is used by many schoolchildren today. To find this collection, enter the APH website, select "Perspectives," followed by "View Our Collection of Mechanical Writers."

## www.nfb.org

This is the website of the National Federation of the Blind. One of the items in the table of contents is called, "How Do You . . . ? Questions Kids Ask." You'll find lots of fascinating information about how people who are blind handle everyday tasks like cooking, shopping, labeling clothes, crossing streets safely, and keeping track of money.

## www.hotbraille.com

This is your chance to send a real braille message (with raised dots!) to someone you know. Simply type your message in print, and Hotbraille will transcribe it and send it in the regular mail to wherever you want. You can specify whether you'd like your message in uncontracted or contracted braille. This website also includes some fun interactive braille games.

# More Reading . . .

Would you like to know more about Louis Braille, the inventor of the braille code, and Helen Keller who was both blind and deaf? You can read short biographies of these two famous people on pages 26-28 of this book. Here are some suggestions for further reading about Louis Braille and Helen Keller. Look for these books at your local library or bookstore:

- **A Picture Book of Louis Braille** (1997) and **A Picture Book of Helen Keller** (1991), by David A. Adler. Both biographies have colorful, detailed pictures that help explain the lives of these two very famous people.

- **Out of Darkness: The Story of Louis Braille**, by Russell Freedman (1997). This well-written chapter book transports readers to the early 1800s when people who were blind usually became beggars. It describes how Louis Braille succeeded in inventing the braille code when he was only 15 years old.

- **Helen Keller**, by Margaret Davidson (reissued 1997). Much of this chapter book focuses on Helen Keller's early years with Anne Sullivan, the teacher who persevered until she taught Helen the meaning of language. Photographs of Helen Keller bring the story to life.

People who are blind are also authors! Sally Alexander, who lost her vision when she was a third-grade teacher, especially enjoys writing for children. Here are two of her books:

- **Mom Can't See Me**, by Sally Hobart Alexander (1990). Mrs. Alexander's 9-year-old daughter, Leslie, tells about life with her mother through words and family photographs. You'll learn how Mrs. Alexander uses braille and meet her guide dog, Marit.

- **Do You Remember the Color Blue? And Other Questions Kids Ask About Blindness**, by Sally Hobart Alexander (2000). In this book Mrs. Alexander answers 13 of the most common questions that kids ask her about her blindness.

Those of you who prefer fiction may enjoy reading some of the books listed below. Each of these books has a character who is blind or has low vision.

## Picture Books

- **Sing to the Stars**, by Mary Brigid Barrett (1994). Ephram, a young violinist, and "Flash Fingers Washington," a jazz pianist who hasn't played since losing his sight, help each other create a special performance.

- **Through Grandpa's Eyes**, by Patricia MacLachlan (1980). A young boy experiences the world as his blind grandfather does using his senses of touch, smell, taste, and hearing.

- **Mandy Sue Day**, by Roberta Karim (1994). Mandy Sue's family gives their daughter a "special day," which she chooses to spend with her horse, Ben.

- **The Seeing Stick**, by Jane Yolen (1997). The Chinese emperor's daughter is blind and sorrowful, but a mysterious visitor helps her learn to see in a new way.

- **Knots on a Counting Rope**, by Bill Martin, Jr., and John Archambault (1987). A Native American boy who is blind talks with his grandfather about his birth, his naming, and his growing skill as a horseman. He learns that courage and love will help him "cross the dark mountain" of his blindness.

## Chapter Books

- **The Cay**, by Theodore Taylor (1969). A 12-year-old boy named Phillip loses his vision and becomes stranded on a deserted island after the Germans torpedo the freighter he was traveling on during World War II. His only companion is Timothy, an elderly black man whose patience and determination help Phillip adjust to his blindness and ultimately survive.

- **The Seeing Summer**, by Jeannette Eyerly (1981). Ten-year-old Carey is excited about meeting the new girl next door until she discovers Jenny is blind. After a shaky start, their friendship grows. Then the girls are kidnapped and must use all their ingenuity to escape from their captors.

- **The Storyteller's Beads**, by Jane Kurtz (1998). Two Ethiopian girls of different cultures flee famine and war in their country. Rahel, who is blind, and Sahay must overcome their prejudices and support each other in order to survive a perilous journey.

- **Sees Behind Trees**, by Michael Dorris (1996). The main character in this book is a Native American boy with low vision who lives in the 16th century. After earning his adult name, "Sees Behind Trees," he embarks on a dangerous quest with an elderly tribal artist.

## How about a job working with people who are blind or visually impaired?

If you think you might enjoy teaching children or adults who are blind or visually impaired, there are several different careers to choose from:

## Teacher of Students with Visual Impairments

These teachers may work with students ages 2 through 21 in a number of different settings. Some students attend special schools, some attend schools in their neighborhood, and some go to special classes for part of the day. Teachers of visually impaired students work both with students who are totally blind and read braille, like Karl (see page 1), and with students who have low vision. They teach braille and many other skills, such as using computers with voice or braille output.

Photo by Nolan Hulsey, courtesy of American Foundation for the Blind

## Orientation and Mobility Specialist

Photo by Natalie Isaak Knott

Nearly everyone recognizes the white cane that people who are blind use to travel safely. But did you know that there are teachers who provide special instruction in travel skills, including the use of the cane? Orientation and mobility (O&M) instructors help children or adults learn their way around their school, neighborhood, or workplace. They train them to cross streets, take public transportation (like buses and the subway), and use proper cane techniques so they arrive at their destinations safely and independently.

## Rehabilitation Teacher

There are actually many more adults who are blind or visually impaired than children. Perhaps you know an older person, such as a grandparent, who has vision problems. A rehabilitation teacher usually works with adults or teens to help them learn everyday tasks such as shopping, cooking, and keeping track of money. They may also teach braille to people who are no longer able to read print.

## Braille Transcriber

Children and adults who use braille at school or on the job depend on braille transcribers for many of their books and other materials. The transcriber's job is to translate print materials into braille and to proofread it to make sure there are no mistakes.

Long ago transcribers used a slate and stylus to produce braille. Now they can use a wide range of computer technology, that lets them work faster, correct mistakes more easily, and produce more than one copy at a time. Transcribers must be certified by the Library of Congress to make sure they have learned all the rules of the braille code. There are additional certification requirements to become a transcriber of music or math materials.

If you would like to help people learn special skills
that will make them more independent,
one of these careers may be right for you!

# Quiz Yourself!

Try answering these questions before and after you read this book.
How much have you learned? Answers are on page 41.

## True or False?

_____ 1. The braille cell has six dots.

_____ 2. Louis Braille was born in France and invented braille when he grew up.

_____ 3. It costs a lot of money to send heavy braille books through the mail.

_____ 4. Special signs called contractions make braille words shorter.

_____ 5. You could hold a sixth-grade braille math book in one hand.

_____ 6. It is faster to read raised-print letters than braille dots.

_____ 7. Tactile graphics help students understand diagrams in math.

_____ 8. There is a braille code for Japanese.

_____ 9. When you write braille with a slate and stylus, you begin punching dots on the right side of the paper.

_____ 10. Miniature braille numbers are used on braille watches.

_____ 11. There are two braille alphabets just like in print, one for lower-case letters and one for upper-case letters.

_____ 12. The numbers in braille math problems are different from the numbers in a braille literature book.

## Secret Message

The Braille Bug has prepared a secret message for you. Now that you've learned so much about braille, see if you can read the message on the braille page that came with this book. Use the braille alphabet on page 3 to help you. Answer is on page 41.

# Braille Worksheet Answers

**Follow the Braille Trails** (page 7)

Path 1: Braille is fun.

Path 2: I love to read.

Path 3: Read with me.

**Match It!** (page 15)

skateboard     earthquake     football     birthday

watermelon     rattlesnake     touchdown

**Sports Scramble** (page 16)

1. soccer
2. swimming
3. bowling
4. biking
5. track
6. baseball
7. wrestling
8. skiing
9. goalball

ALL these sports, with some modifications, are enjoyed by people who are blind. In fact, soccer is the most popular sport worldwide for blind athletes. Many children and adults who are blind enjoy tandem biking. Beep baseball is played with two beeping bases and a beeping ball on a tee. In goalball, a sport specifically designed for blind players, participants block a fast-moving ball containing a bell with their bodies, often stretching out full length on the floor.

**Riddles** (page 17)

1. a rainbow
2. noon
3. take off the s
4. parachute school
5. Bugs Bunny
6. your shoe
7. holes
8. it is too tired
9. a skating rink
10. bring a chair back with you

# Braille Puzzle Answers

## Solution to Word Search (page 30)

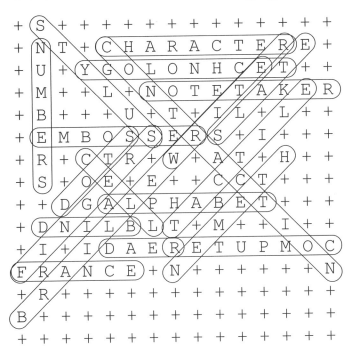

## Secret Message (on braille page)
### A Braille Contest

You will need 2 teams of 7 players. Give paper plates to 6 players on each team. Have the six players stand in 2 rows of 3, like the dots in a braille cell. The seventh player is the coach. Ask your teacher to call out the name of a letter. The first team to hold up the dots for that letter is the winner.

## Solution to Crossword Puzzle (page 31)

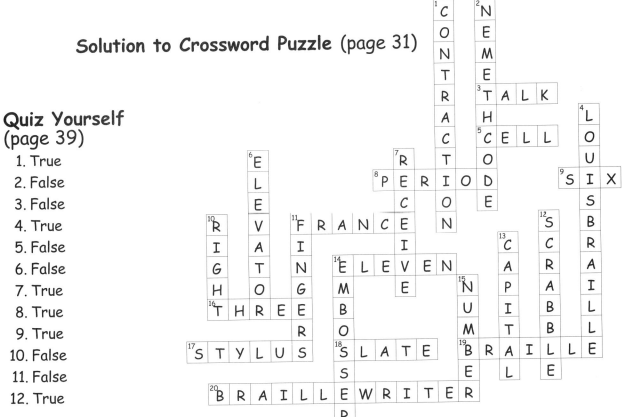

## Quiz Yourself
### (page 39)

1. True
2. False
3. False
4. True
5. False
6. False
7. True
8. True
9. True
10. False
11. False
12. True

# Visit me on the Web!

www.afb.org/braillebug